THAT'S OUR GYM TEACHER!

The author and photographer wish to thank the children and faculty at P.S. 290, The Manhattan New School, for their wonderful help and inspiration in the preparation of this book. Special thanks to Stephen Brown for all his wonderful help and support in the preparation of the manuscript.

Library of Congress Cataloging-in-Publication Data
Morris, Ann, 1930-
That's our gym teacher!/Ann Morris; photographs and illustrations by Peter Linenthal.
p. cm.—(That's our school)
Summary: Introduces Michael Miller, an elementary school gym teacher, describing what he does during the school day and how he interacts with other staff and students.
ISBN 0-7613-2403-8 (lib. bdg.)
1. Physical education for children—Juvenile literature. 2. Physical education teachers—Juvenile literature. [1. Physical education teachers. 2. Occupations. 3. Physical education and training]
I. Linenthal, Peter, ill.   II. Title.
GV443.M64   2003
372.86—dc21   2002155132

The Millbrook Press, Inc.
2 Old New Milford Road
Brookfield, Connecticut 06804
www.millbrookpress.com

THAT'S OUR GYM TEACHER!

Ann Morris

**Photographs and Illustrations
by Peter Linenthal**

The Millbrook Press / Brookfield, Connecticut

A gym teacher teaches children how to make their bodies stronger and healthier. He teaches them how to play different sports and the rules for these games. And he teaches them how to have fun! Michael Miller is our gym teacher, and he does all of these things. He's really cool!

Our gym teacher teaches us all kinds of games and other activities.

We learn how to be good sports and how to do things we never thought we could.

We learn how to have fun with each other and how to help each other.

Sometimes we play ball on a special street outside our school where there are no moving cars. Our crossing guard directs the cars away from the street so that we can play safely.

Sometimes our gym teacher
lets us run in the courtyard
behind our school.
He says that running
strengthens our muscles and
makes our hearts stronger.

Mr. Miller also talks to us
about staying healthy.
He says it's very important
for us to eat good food and to
get lots of sleep and exercise.

In gym class, our teacher
prepares us for our fitness test.
The test checks how well
our bodies are working.
We do lots of strengthening exercises.
"Arms up," Mr. Miller says.
Then, "Slowly, down."

We do airplanes . . .
and jumping jacks . . .
and push-ups.
All these exercises help
make us better players.
And they keep our
hearts and muscles
strong and our bodies
growing healthy.

We also do stretching exercises.
They help to keep our bodies
limber and flexible.

Our gym teacher is very fair.

He needs to be fair because he is the "referee."

He keeps the score when we play.

We learn that rules are for everyone.

"Always try your best," says Mr. Miller.

When we learn how to do our best

we feel good about ourselves.

Some of us don't have fathers at home,

so he is like a good father to us.

When we do well, he says "great job!"

or "give me five!"

Mr. Miller often meets with our principal to plan activities. Sometimes they plan field days, when we go to the park and play all kinds of games. Sometimes they plan class trips or parents' nights.

Mr. Miller also
meets with other
teachers to plan
special lessons
or activities.

Mr. Miller grew up with two younger sisters, Jodi and Robin, who share his love of sports.

Mr. Miller as a boy with his parents and sisters

When he was a boy,
he loved playing soccer,
baseball, basketball,
hockey, and tennis.
He also liked to bike
and hike and swim.
Later he learned roller
blading and snowboarding.
"I always liked sports,"
he told us. "That's why
I became a gym teacher."

Mr. Miller at his synagogue

But Mr. Miller does more than teach gym. He is always busy. He also works in a shelter helping people who do not have a place to live. And he helps out at his synagogue—greeting people and showing them where to sit.

He especially enjoys spending time with his wife, Tara, and their dog, Codey. Mr. Miller and his wife do many things together—gardening, shopping, exercising, taking care of the house, meeting with friends, and taking vacations.

On weekends, our gym teacher and his wife go to Fire Island, a small island near New York City. They have a house and a restaurant there, Michael's Ristorante. "Ristorante" means restaurant in Italian. Mr. Miller is in charge of the restaurant and Mrs. Miller is the business manager.

Behind his beach house, Mr. Miller grows vegetables and beautiful plants for his restaurant and for his home. Mr. Miller's restaurant means a lot to him. He thinks he's lucky to have two jobs— COOK and TEACHER.

Once some of us visited our gym teacher at his restaurant. He taught us to make pizza. He says that eating healthy food makes you feel good. When the pizza was done, we had a pizza party. We think we're very lucky. Whoever heard of a great gym teacher who could also make the *best* pizza?

THINGS TO DO

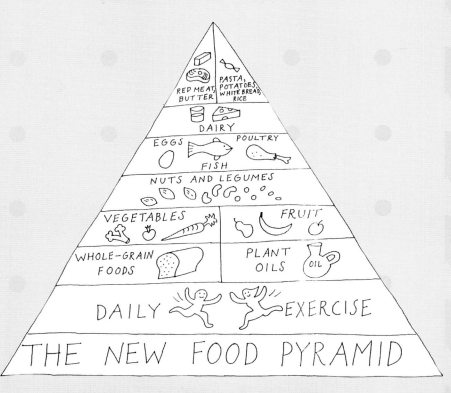

Make a Food Poster

**Make a poster showing things
that are good for you to eat.**

Be a Gym Teacher

- **Take turns being referee at a baseball or
other ball game.**

- **Lead your class in some exercises.**

Make Pizza

Making pizza is easy. Use Mr. Miller's recipe.

Michael's Pizza Serves 8.

Here is what you need:

1 bag prepared pizza dough	2 pinches sugar
12 ounce can chopped plum tomatoes	2 teaspoons garlic powder
4 tablespoons olive oil	2 pinches oregano
4 basil leaves, chopped	1 handful grated Romano cheese
2 pinches salt	12 ounces grated mozzarella cheese
1 pinch ground black pepper	

Here is what you do:

Preheat the oven to 450°F. To make the crust, press the dough into a 12-inch round shape or roll it out on a floured board. Spread half the olive oil on a cookie sheet or a pizza stone and place the crust on it. To make the sauce, pour tomatoes in a bowl. Add the remaining olive oil, chopped basil, salt, pepper, sugar, and garlic powder. Mix until blended. Pour the sauce over the uncooked pizza crust. Sprinkle the mozzarella cheese evenly over the sauce. Top with oregano and Romano cheese. Have an adult help you put your pie in the oven. Bake until edges are brown, 10-12 minutes. Cut into eight pieces and serve.

About the Author

Ann Morris loves children, and she loves writing books
for children. She has written more than eighty books for
children, including a series of books for The Millbrook
Press about grandmothers and their grandchildren called
What Was It Like, Grandma? For many years Ann Morris
taught school. Eventually, she left teaching to become
an editor with a children's book publishing company.
While she still sometimes teaches workshops and
seminars for teachers, Ann Morris now spends most
of her time writing. She lives in New York City.

About the Photographer-Illustrator

Peter Linenthal is a talented photographer and illustrator.
He studied fine arts at the San Francisco Art Institute.
He is a native of California and teaches at the San Francisco
Center for the Book. Peter Linenthal also loves children
and working on books for children. He did the photographs
and illustrations for Ann Morris's books about grandmothers.